I0006781

Puzzles in Java

Shaping Beginners

Kathiravan Udayakumar

Order this book online at www.trafford.com
or email orders@trafford.com

Most Trafford titles are also available at major online book retailers.

Printed in the United States of America.

ISBN: 978-1-4669-8885-9 (sc)
ISBN: 978-1-4669-8882-8 (e)

Trafford rev. 05/13/2013

www.trafford.com

North America & international
toll-free: 1 888 232 4444 (USA & Canada)
phone: 250 383 6864 • fax: 812 355 4082

This book is dedicated to my parents
Dr. P. Udayakumar & Dr. K. Mangayarkarasi

About the Author

Kathiravan Udayakumar, Senior Architect-Technology, has 9 years of IT experience with expertise in Oracle Fusion Middleware Products and PeopleSoft Applications. All of his experience relates to World's First Implementation (Green-field) IT System Implementation and System Integration. Kathir holds his Bachelor Degree as a Gold Medalist in Electronics and Communication Engineering from Madurai Kamaraj University, a Master of Science Degree in System Software Engineering from Birla Institute of Science and Technology, Pilani and a Master of Business Administration Degree in Sales and Marketing from Symbiosis Institute, Pune. He has extensive experience in architecting and designing solutions using various Oracle Fusion and PeopleSoft Products. Kathir works for a highly reputed IT Consulting Organization and is considered to be key member of the Fusion COE team. Kathir has trained close to 100+ Associates in Fusion Middleware 11g to gain the skills for developing and designing solutions using Oracle SOA Suite 11g.

This is sixth international book from the author; first book was published in May 2012 by Packt Publishing, titled Oracle SOA Infrastructure Implementation Certification Handbook (1Z0-451). Second one was published in Sep 2012 by Trafford Publishing,titled "Oracle SOA Patterns", thrid was published in Oct 2012 by Trafford Publishing titled "Oracle SOA Frameworks" and fourth, "Hello World" to Oracle SOA.

Acknowledgment

I like to thank our family and friends who have supported me during the course of this work. I also like to thank Trafford Publishing accepting to publish my work. Especially, we like to thank Greg, Earl and Nick from Trafford Publishing to make this book a successful edition.

Preface

Puzzles in Java is a preliminary tool for the Beginners in Java to test their skills and get an in depth knowledge of the core Java. This Book consists of 299 unique Puzzles that will help readers to. Answers to puzzles can be identified using the Game Codes provided in the beginning of the book. This book encourages the readers to execute the puzzles in JDK to identify the results and understand details of the puzzles. Reader should note each puzzle provided in the book should be compiled as independent classes to get the results.

Game Codes

1. When JVM Executes a class file it looks for the following method to start the main thread public static void main (String args [])

   The argument variable specified in its main should be a string variable which means public static void main (String a []) is 100% acceptable.

2. The Compiler expects class not Class, it is a class you can use it inside a class or method

3. Keywords & Reserved words cannot be used as variables

4. Data type supported by java are int, byte, short, long, float, double and char.

5. Assignment of higher values (i.e. value outside the range of the data type) may result in the loss of precision

6. Variable must be declared, before it is used

7. Array elements should be accessed through index value. The value of the index is within the range of value it stores

8. Non static variable and methods cannot be used with in the static context

9. All the Methods specified in the class must specify its return type in its signature

10. Final variable must be initialized when it is declared or in constructor

11. Variables declared within the Method can be either static or default (no qualifier)

12. We cannot convert the String to integer by (down) conversion process; we have to use parseInt method to convert to int.

13. Arithmetic operation cannot be performed on Boolean variable

14. We cannot assign null to primitive data types

15. We cannot call main method in any of the method unless we override the public static void main (String args [ ])

16. System.out.println ( ) does not return any value.

17. We cannot declare the Variable as void as we do in C for Pointers.

18. Final variable can be assigned only once when it is declared in constructor or in static block.

19. Static final variable must be initialized when it is declared.

20. In Java, we don't have the concept of Global variables, all the variables and methods must be defined within the class.

21. Data type must be specified for a variable when declared

22. Abstract keyword is used to qualify a class or method

23. Static Qualifier can be applied to block of code ,method or class

24. A class can be qualified with public or default (no access specifier)

25. We cannot use static qualifier in method parameter

26. Value of final variable cannot be changed.

27. Changing the qualifier in defining the methods does not mean overriding the method, we are only changing the scope of the method, however we cannot have two method with similar signature and different scope.

28. Loss of precision occurs if you assign the out of range value to the variable.

29. Shift Operators can be applied to integer data types

30. Abstract method cannot be declared within the non abstract class

31. Abstract method cannot have body

32. Abstract class can contain non abstract method but non abstract class cannot contain abstract method.

33. Objects cannot be created for abstract classes

34. abstract and static keyword cannot be used in combination.

35. We can't invoke a constructor through an object; It is executed when an object is created.

36. Output may vary from Compiler to compiler. The Object information can be displayed by Overriding toString ( ) method in the class.

37. We cannot assign value to primitive data types using new operator

38. println (java.lang.String,int) method is not defined in System.out Package.

39. When we compare two references with == it compares whether both references refers to same Object not with value of the Object it contains, to do it we need to compare using equals method.

40. (+) Operator can be used only with String Objects

41. &&, || ,! Operators can be applied only to boolean data type.

42. Boolean is a class and boolean is a data type.

43. Variable must be assigned a value before it is accessed

44. synchronized qualifier cannot be applied to variable, it can be applied either to method or block of code.

45. Arithmetic operators cannot be applied to boolean data types

46. final is different from finally, finally is applied to block of code.

47. Constant expression is required within Switch block.

48. Duplicate case cannot be used in same switch block.

49. float ,boolean, double values cannot be used in switch expression. Switch expression can handle only int or char.

50. continue statement can be used only within the loop .

51. finally block cannot exist without try block

52. child class reference cannot refer Parent class Object

53. super keyword cannot be used in static context.

54. Method Declared as final in parent class cannot be overridden by child class

55. We cannot extend a class with private constructor

56. We cannot make a constructor as final.

57. Call to this( ) must be first statement in Constructor

58. When we extend a class from another class, the super class must provide the same constructor signatures as in the child classes. Why this occurs ?, The child class constructor adds super() internally to ever constructor in its class, so it looks for the constructor in the super class with the same signature.

59. String class does not have append & reverse function defined in it.

60. We cannot extend a final class

61. We cannot use the method of down casting from higher value to lower value through when converting data from Double to Float because they are classes. We must use the functions provided in the class to convert from one class to other class.

62. Inner class cannot have static declaration.

63. Objects cannot be created for Interfaces and Abstract Classes

64. Interface method are always abstract methods

65. class that implements an interface should not apply a weaker privilege to function we implemented in classes

66. > ,>=,<,<= operators are not overloaded by default for String Object.

67. this, this() key word cannot be referenced in static context.

68. Super class reference can refer the sub class object; but it cannot not access the subclass properties.

69. When we create an array of Objects, we are only qualifying the reference to hold the array of objects. We have to initialize them.

70. When we override a method we should not apply a weaker access privileges to that method, which may result in compile time error.

71. We cannot use any other qualifier other than final for Local variable.

72. Constructor cannot use static as Qualifier with it.

73. When we invoke an overridden method using the super class reference, it invokes the super class method, because at compile it checks the access right; but at runtime, it runs the subclass overridden method.

74. Recursive constructor invocation is not allowed in java

75. Each and Ever class created extends Object class.

76. The array objects are different from primitive data types

77. We cannot have two different functions with same signature and different access control in same class. This also applies to inherited classes.

78. interface & final modifier cannot occur together (We can never make an interface final)

79. Only an interface can extend an interface, a class can only implement an interface.

80. When we specify the variable in an interface as static, we need to initialize the value explicitly; however in class the value is automatically initialized to 0 for static variables.

81. Default arguments (argument with value initialized) feature is not available in java.

82. Method with no body should be declared as abstract method.

Puzzle in Java

Puzzle 1:

```
class Puzzle1
{
        public static void main (String args [])
        {
        System.out.println ("Nice Way to Begin");
        }
}
```

Puzzle 2:

```
class Puzzle2
{
        public static void main ( )
        {
        int a =9;
        System.out.println ("a is" +a);
        }
}
```

Puzzle 3:

```
class Puzzle3
{
        public static void main ( int a[] )
```

```
        {
        System.out.println ("I am in main");
        }
}
```

Puzzle 4:

```
Class Puzzle4
{
        public static void main ( String args [] )
        {
        System.out.println (args[0]+" "+args[1]);
        }
}
```

Puzzle 5:

```
class Puzzle5
{
        public void main ( String args [] )
        {
        }
}
```

Puzzle 6:

```
class Puzzle6
{
        public void static main ( String args [] )
        {
        }
}
```

Puzzle 7:

```
class Puzzle7
{
        public static int main ( String args [] )
        {
        }
}
```

Puzzle 8:

```
class Puzzle8
{
        private static void main ( String args [] )
        {
        }
}
```

Puzzle 9:

```
class Puzzle9
{
        public static void main(String args[])
        {
        int a=5,b=3;
        }
}
```

Puzzle 10:

```
class Puzzle10
{
        public static void main(String args[])
        {
```

```
        int static=4;
        float Double=5;
        Double Char=3;
        System.out.println(static +” “+Double+” “+Char);
        }
}
```

Puzzle 11:

```
class Puzzle11
{
        public static void main(String args[]){
        int a=010, b=0x10, a1=010;
        float c=010;
        long double b1=010.00d;
        System.out.println(“a”+a+”b”+b+”c”+c+”a1”+a1+”b1”+b1);
        }
}
```

Puzzle 12:

```
class Puzzle12
{
        public static void main(String args[]){
        float b=010;
        double c=010d;
        System.out.println(“F”+b+”D”+c);
        }
}
```

Puzzle 13:

```
class Puzzle13
{
```

```
        public static void main(String args[]){
        byte a=4,c=127;
        int b=a, d=c;
        System.out.println("a is "+a+"b is "+b);}
}
```

Puzzle 14:

```
class Puzzle14
{
        public static void main(String args[])
        {
        char c='a';
        int b=c;
        double a=b;
        float d=b;
        System.out.println(a+" "+b+" "+c+" "+d);
        }
}
```

Puzzle 15:

```
class Puzzle15
{
        public static void main(String args[])
        {
        float a=10.0;
        System.out.println("float"+a);
        }
}
```

Puzzle 16:

```
class Puzzle16
```

```
{
        public static void main(String args[])
        {
        int a=b=6;
        }
}
```

Puzzle 17:

```
class Puzzle17
{
        public static void main(String args[]){
        char c='a';
        int b=c;
        double a=b;
        float d=a;
        System.out.println(a+b+c+d);
        }
}
```

Puzzle 18:

```
class Puzzle18
{
        public static void main(String args[])
        {
        int a[] = new int[4];
        int b[] = new int[4];
        int c[] ={1,4,3,2};
        b=c;
        a=c;
        System.out.println(a+b+c+d);
        }
}
```

Puzzle 19:

```
class Puzzle19
{         int a;
          public static void main(String args[]){
          System.out.println(a);}
}
```

Puzzle 20:

```
class Puzzle20
{
          public static void main(String args[])
          {
          int a[] =new int [100];
          for(int i=0;i<100;i++)
          System.out.println("Be"+a[i]);
          }
}
```

Puzzle 21:

```
abstract class Puzzle21A
{
          Puzzle21A( )
          {
          System.out.println("I am in abstract A");
          }
          void B( )
          {
          System.out.println("I am in abstract B");
          }
}
```

```
class Puzzle21B extends Puzzle21B
{
        public static void main(String args[])
        {
        new B( );
        }
}
```

Puzzle 22:

```
abstract class Puzzle22A
{
        Puzzle22A( ){
        System.out.println("I am in abstract A");}
        B( ){
        System.out.println("I am in abstract B");}
}
class Puzzle22B extends Puzzle22B
{
        public static void main(String args[]){
        B( );
        }
}
```

Puzzle 23:

```
class Puzzle23A
{
        private int a=9;
        public static int get_a(){
        return a;}
}
class Puzzle23B extends Puzzle23A
{
```

```
        public static void main(String args[])
        {
        int b;
        b=get_a();
        System.out.println(b);
        }
}
```

Puzzle 24:

```
class Puzzle24
{
        protected int geta()
        {
        return a;
        }
}
```

Puzzle 25:

```
class Puzzle25
{
        final int a;
        Puzzle25()
        {
        a=9;
        System.out.println("Sliver Puzzle...");
        }
        public static void main(String args[])
        {
        Puzzle25 P25 =new Puzzle25();
        }
}
```

Puzzle 26:

```
public class Puzzle26
{
        int i;
        public static void main(String args[])
        {
        System.out.println(a=4);
        }
}
```

Puzzle 27:

```
class Puzzle27
{
        int i;
        public static void main(String args[])
        {
        System.out.println('A'>64);
        }
}
```

Puzzle 28:

```
class Puzzle28
{
        public static void main(String args[])
        {
        private int i;
        System.out.println(i);
        }
}
```

Puzzle 29:

```
class Puzzle29
{
        public int i=2;
        public static void main(String args[])
        {
        int i;
        System.out.println(i);
        }
}
```

Puzzle 30:

```
class Puzzle30
{
        public static void main(String a[])
        {
        System.out.println((int)a[0]+(int)a[1]);
        }
}
```

Puzzle 31:

```
class Puzzle31
{
        public static void main(String args[])
        {
        System.out.println("Hai"+4+3);
        }
}
```

Puzzle 32:

```
class Puzzle32
{
	public static void main(String args[])
	{
	System.out.println(null+4+3);
	}
}
```

Puzzle 33:

```
class Puzzle33
{
	public static void main(String args[])
	{
	System.out.println(true+4+3);
	}
}
```

Puzzle 34:

```
class Puzzle34
{
	public static void main(String args[])
	{
	System.out.println(4+3+null);
	}
}
```

Puzzle 35:

```
class Puzzle35
{
```

```
	public static void main(String args[])
	{
	System.out.println(null+false);
	}
}
```

Puzzle 36:

```
class Puzzle36
{
	public static void main(String args[])
	{
	int j;
	j=true|false;
	System.out.println(j);
	}
}
```

Puzzle 37:

```
class Puzzle37
{
	public static void main(String args[])
	{
	int Null=null;
	System.out.println(Null);
	}
}
```

Puzzle 38:

```
class Puzzle38
{
	public static void main(String args[])
```

```
        {
        System.out.println(null);
        }
}
```

Puzzle 39:

```
class Puzzle39
{
        void main( )
        {
        System.out.println("I am in void main");
        }
        public static void main(String args[])
        {
        Puzzle39 P39= new Puzzle39( );
        P39.main( );
        }
}
```

Puzzle 40:

```
class Puzzle40
{
        public static void main(String args[])
        {
        Puzzle40 P40 = new Puzzle40( );
        P40.main( );
        }
}
```

Puzzle 41:

```
class Puzzle41
```

```
{
        public static void main(String args[]){
        Puzzle41 P41 = new Puzzle41( );
        P41.main("Rama" );
        }
}
```

Puzzle 42:

```
class Puzzle42
{
        void main( String args[]){
        System.out.println("main" + args[0]);
        }
        public static void main(String args[]){
        Puzzle42 P42 = new Puzzle42( );
        P42.main("Best" );
        }
}
```

Puzzle 43:

```
class Puzzle43
{
        void Puzzle43A( ){
        main("Rest", "Best");
        }
        public static void main(String args[]){
        Puzzle43 P43 = new Puzzle43( );
        P43. Puzzle43A ( );
        }
}
```

Puzzle 44:

```
class Puzzle44
{
        public static void main(String args[]){
        int j;
        j=System.out.println("Hello"+ args[0]);
        }
}
```

Puzzle 45:

```
class Puzzle45
{
        public static void main(String args[])
        {
        void j;
        j=System.out.println();
        }
}
```

Puzzle 46:

```
class Puzzle46
{
        final int j;
        public static void main(String args[])
        {
        System.out.println("How it is "+j);
        }
}
```

Puzzle 47:

```
class Puzzle47
{
        final int j=1;
        public void main(String args[])
        {
        System.out.println("How it is "+j);
        }
}
```

Puzzle 48:

```
class Puzzle48
{
        final int j=4;
        Puzzle48( )
        {
        j=5;
        }
        public static void main(String args[])
        {
        Puzzle48 o =new Puzzle48( );
        System.out.println("How it is "+o.j);
        }
}
```

Puzzle 49:

```
class Puzzle49
{
        static final int j;
        Puzzle49()
        {
```

```
        j=5;
        }
        public static void main(String args[ ])
        {
        Puzzle49 o =new Puzzle49 ();
        System.out.println("How it is "+o.j);
        }
}
```

Puzzle 50:

```
class Puzzle50
{
        static final int j=50;

        public static void main(String args[ ])
        {
        System.out.println("Golden hit" + j);
        }
}
```

Puzzle 51:

```
class Puzzle51
{
        final static int j=51;
        public static void main(String args[])
        {
        Puzzle51 o =new Puzzle51();
        Puzzle51 o1 =new Puzzle51();
        System.out.print(o.j+" ");
        System.out.print(" "+Puzzle51.j+" ");
        System.out.println(j);
        }
}
```

Puzzle 52:

```
class Puzzle52
{
        final int j;

        Puzzle52(int k){
        j=k;
        }

        public static void main(String args[])
        {
        Puzzle51 o =new Puzzle51(2);
        Puzzle51 o1 =new Puzzle51(3);
        System.out.print(o.j+" ");
        System.out.print(o1.j);
        }
}
```

Puzzle 53:

```
int i;
class Puzzle53
{
        public static void main(String args[])
        {
        System.out.println(i);
        }
}
```

Puzzle 54:

```
class Puzzle54
{
```

```
        public static void main(String args[]){
        g();
        }
        static void g(){
        System.out.println("I am in static g() ")
        b();
        }
        void b(){
        System.out.println("I am in static b() ")
        }
}
```

Puzzle 55:

```
class Puzzle55
{
        public static void main(String args[])
        {
        public a;
        a=5;
        System.out.println(a);
        }
}
```

Puzzle 56:

```
class Puzzle56
{
        public static void main(String args[])
        {
        abstract int j;
        System.out.println(j);
        }
}
```

Puzzle 57:

```
class Puzzle56
{
        public static void main(String args[])
        {
        transient int j;
        System.out.println(j);
        }
}
```

Puzzle 58:

```
class Puzzle58
{
        public static void main(String args[])
        {
        strictfp int j;
        System.out.println(j);
        }
}
```

Puzzle 59:

```
Private class Puzzle59
{
        public static void main(String args[])
        {
        System.out.println("Enjoying...");
        }
}
```

Puzzle 60:

```
class Puzzle60
{
        static int main=5;
        public static void main(String args[])
        {
        System.out.println(main);
        }
}
```

Puzzle 61:

```
class Puzzle61
{
        public static void main(String args[])
        {
        final int main =1;
        System.out.println(main);
        }
}
```

Puzzle 62:

```
class Puzzle62
{
        void g(int x, int y){
        System.out.println("X is "+x+ " Y is "+ y);
        }
}
```

Puzzle 63:

```
class Puzzle63
```

```
{
        void display(static int x, int y){
        System.out.println("X is "+x+ " Y is "+ y);
        }
        public static void main(String args[]){
        Puzzle63 o = new Puzzle63();
        o.display(1,2);
        }
}
```

Puzzle 64:

```
class Puzzle64
{
        void display(final int x, int y){
        System.out.println("X is "+x+ " Y is "+ y);
        }
        public static void main(String args[]){
        Puzzle64 o = new Puzzle64();
        o.display(1,2);
        }
}
```

Puzzle 65:

```
class Puzzle65
{
        static void display(){
        System.out.print("Hai"+" ");
        }
        public static void main(String args[]){
        Puzzle65 o = new Puzzle65();
        o.display();
        Puzzle65.display();
```

```
        }
}
```

Puzzle 66:

```
class Puzzle66
{
        void display(final int i, int k){
        System.out.println("J&K" are +j + k);
        j++; k++;
        System.out.println("J&K" are +j + k);}
}
```

Puzzle 67:

```
class Puzzle67
{
        public static void main(String args[]){
        int j=5;
        short k=2;
        int l=j<<k;
        System.out.println(l);
        }
}
```

Puzzle 68:

```
class Puzzle68
{
        static void display()
        {
        System.out.print("Hai"+" ");
        }
        void display()
```

```
        {
        System.out.print("Hai"+" ");
        }
        public static void main(String args[])
        {
        Puzzle65 o = new Puzzle65();
        o.display();
        Puzzle65.display();
        }
}
```

Puzzle 69:

```
class Puzzle69
{
        public static void main(String args[]){
        short j=5;
        int k=2;
        short l=j<<k;
        System.out.println(l);
        }
}
```

Puzzle 70:

```
class Puzzle70
{
        public static void main(String args[]){
        final int j=2,k=3;
        k++;
        System.out.println(k);
        }
}
```

Puzzle 71:

```
class Puzzle71
{
        public static void main(String args[]){
        final int j=2;
        int k=j<<3;
        System.out.println(k);
        }
}
```

Puzzle 72:

```
class Puzzle72
{
        public static void main(String args[]){
        int k=0xffffffff;
        System.out.println(k);
        }
}
```

Puzzle 73:

```
class Puzzle73
{
        public static void main(String args[]){
        double k=2;
        int j=3;
        System.out.println(j<<k);
        }
}
```

Puzzle 74:

```
class Puzzle74
{
        public static void main(String args[]){
        int k=0x0ffffff;
        k>>>=k;
        System.out.println(k);
        }
}
```

Puzzle 75:

```
class Puzzle75
{
        public static void main(String args[]){
        int y=0x16;
        System.out.println(y/06);
        }
}
```

Puzzle 76:

```
class Puzzle76
{
        public static void main(String args[]){
        int x=-2,y=3;
        System.out.println(y<<3);
        }
}
```

Puzzle 77:

```
class Puzzle77
```

```
{
	public static void main(String args[]){
	int x=0x80000008;
	System.out.println(x>>4);
	System.out.println(x>>>=4);
	System.out.println(x>4);
	}
}
```

Puzzle 78:

```
class Puzzle78
{
	public static void main(String args[]){
	int a=0x12,b=012,c=12;
	System.out.println(a/c);
	System.out.println(b/c);
	System.out.println(a/b);
	}
}
```

Puzzle 79:

```
class Puzzle79
{
	public static void main(String args[]){
	int a=0x12,b=012,c=12;
	float x=(float)a/b, y=(float)b/c;
	System.out.println(x);
	System.out.println(y);
	}
}
```

Puzzle 80:

```
class Puzzle80
{
	public static void main(String args[]){
	Puzzle80 o =new Puzzle80();
	o.main();
	}
	abstract void main(){
	System.out.println("I am in abstract fun")
	}
}
```

Puzzle 81:

```
abstract class Puzzle81
{
	public static void main(String args[]){
	System.out.println("I am in abstract");
	}
}
```

Puzzle 82:

```
abstract class Puzzle82
{
	abstract void main();

	public static void main(String args[])
	{
	System.out.println("I am in abstract");
	}
}
```

Puzzle 83:

```
abstract class Puzzle83
{
        static int j=10;
        Puzzle83()
        {
        j++;
        }
        public static void main(String args[])
        {
        new Puzzle83();
        new Puzzle83();
        System.out.println(j);
        }
}
```

Puzzle 84:

```
class Puzzle84A
{
        static int j=0;
        Puzzle84A()
        {
        j++;
        }
}

class Puzzle84B extends Puzzle84A
{
        public static void main(String args[])
        {
        new Puzzle84A();
        new Puzzle84A();
```

```
        System.out.println(j);
        }
}
```

Puzzle 85:

```
abstract class Puzzle85A
{
        abstract void main=0;
}

class Puzzle85B extends Puzzle85A
{
        public static void main(String args[])
        {
        System.out.println("Hello");
        }
}
```

Puzzle 86:

```
abstract class Puzzle86A
{
        abstract public static void main(String args[]);
}

class Puzzle86B extends Puzzle86A
{
        public static void main(String args[])
        {
        System.out.println("Hello");
        }
}
```

Puzzle 87:

```
class Puzzle87
{
        int k;
        Puzzle87(){
        System.out.println("Create Test");}
        Puzzle87(int j){
        k=j;
        System.out.println("Create Test");}
        public static void main(String args[]){
        Puzzle87 P87 =new Puzzle87();
        P87. Puzzle87();
        P87. Puzzle87(5);
        }
}
```

Puzzle 88:

```
class Puzzle88
{
        int k;
        Puzzle88()
        {
        System.out.println("Create Puzzle");
        }
        static void Puzzle88(int j)
        {
        k=j;
        System.out.println("Create void Puzzle");
        }
        public static void main(String args[])
        {
        Puzzle88 P88 =new Puzzle88();
```

```
        P88. Puzzle88();
        P88. Puzzle88(5);
        }
}
```

Puzzle 89:

```
class Puzzle89
{
        public static void main(String args[])
        {
        Puzzle89 P89 = new Puzzle89();
        System.out.println(P89);
        }
}
```

Puzzle 90:

```
class Puzzle90
{
        static int k;

        Puzzle90()
        {
        System.out.println("Create Puzzling");
        }

        Puzzle90(int i)
        {
        k=i;
        System.out.println("Create Puzzle with"+i);
        }

        static int get_k()
```

```
        {
        return k;
        }

public static void main(String args[])
{
        Puzzle90 P90 = new Puzzle90();
        int i;
        i= Puzzle90.get_k();
        System.out.println(" Value of I is "+i);
        new Puzzle90(4);
        System.out.println(Puzzle90.get_k());
        }
}
```

Puzzle 91:

```
class Puzzle91
{
        static int k;
        Puzzle91(){
        System.out.println("Create Puzzle");
        }

        void Puzzle91(){
        System.out.println("Create Puzzle");
        }

        static void Puzzle91(int j){
        k=j;
        System.out.println("Create void Puzzle");
        }

        public static void main(String args[]){
                Puzzle91 P91 =new Puzzle91();
                P91. Puzzle91();
```

```
            P91. Puzzle91(5);
        }
}
```

Puzzle 92:

```
class Puzzle92
{
        public static void main(String args[]){
        Puzzle92 P92 =new Puzzle92();
        System.out.println(new Puzzle92());
        }
}
```

Puzzle 93:

```
class Puzzle93
{
        Puzzle93(){
        System.out.println("Hai");
        }
        public static void main(String args[]){
        System.out.println(new Puzzle93());
        }
}
```

Puzzle 94:

```
class Puzzle94
{
        public static void main(String args[]){
        System.out.println(System.out.println("Ha"));
        }
}
```

Puzzle 95:

```
class Puzzle95
{
	public static void main(String args[]){
	int i;
	i =new int(4);
	System.out.println(i);
	}
}
```

Puzzle 96:

```
class Puzzle96
{
	public static void main(String args[])
	{
	String s=”Good Start”;
	System.out.println(s);
	}
}
```

Puzzle 97:

```
class Puzzle97
{
	public static void main(String args[])
	{
	String s= new String(“Good start”);
	System.out.println(s);
	}
}
```

Puzzle 98:

```
class Puzzle98
{
        public static void main(String args[])
        {
        int i=5;
        System.out.println("I value is %d",i);
        }
}
```

Puzzle 99:

```
class Puzzle99
{
        public static void main(String args[])
        {
        int i=5;
        System.out.println("I value is %d" + i);
        }
}
```

Puzzle 100:

```
class Puzzle100{

        public static void main(String args[])
        {
        String s = new String("Good Luck");
         String t = new String("Good Luck");

        if(s==t)
        System.out.println("They are same"+ s);
        else
```

```
        System.out.println("They are different "+s+ t);
        }
}
```

Puzzle 101:

```
class Puzzle101{

        public static void main(String args[])
        {
        String s = new String("Good Luck");
         String t = s;

        if(s==t)
        System.out.println("They are same"+ s);
        else
        System.out.println("They are different "+s+ t);
        }
}
```

Puzzle 102:

```
class Puzzle102
{
        public static void main(String args[])
        {
        String s = new String("Good Luck");
         String t +=s;
        System.out.println(t);
        }
}
```

Puzzle 103:

```
class Puzzle103{
        public static void main(String args[]){
        String s = new String ("Testing");
        String t=s;
        s=s+ "Java";
        System.out.println(t);
        }
}
```

Puzzle 104:

```
class Puzzle104{
        int i;
        public static void main(String args[]){
        Puzzle104 P104A =new Puzzle104();
        Puzzle104 P104B = P104A;
        P104A.i=7;
        System.out.print(P104B.i);
        P104A.i=3;
        System.out.println(","+ P104B.i);
        }
}
```

Puzzle 105:

```
class Puzzle105{
        public static void main(String args[]){
        String s = null;
        String t=s;
        t= new String("Javaing");
         System.out.println(s);
        }
}
```

Puzzle 106:

```
class Puzzle106{
        public static void main(String args[]){
        int i;
        i=5;
        System.out.print(i++ +”,”);
        System.out.print(--i+”, ”);
        System.out.println(++i-i--);
        }
}
```

Puzzle 107:

```
class Puzzle107{
        public static void main(String args[]){
        int j=4,k;
        k=++j*j--/j;
        System.out.println(k);
        }
}
```

Puzzle 108:

```
class Puzzle108{
        public static void main(String args[]){
        String s =new String(“Java 1.4” );
        s *= “Kawa”;
        System.out.println(“Value of s is ”+s);
        }
}
```

Puzzle 109:

```
class Puzzle109
{
	public static void main (String args [])
	{
	int j=4, k=3;
	double d =j/k+4;
	System.out.println (d);
	}
}
```

Puzzle 110:

```
class Puzzle110
{
	public static void main (String args [])
	{
	int j=4, k=3, l=j&k+4;
	System.out.println (l);
	}
}
```

Puzzle 111:

```
class Puzzle111
{
	public static void main (String args [])
	{
	int j=4, k=4, l=j&&k;
	System.out.println (l);
	}
}
```

Puzzle 112:

```
class Puzzle112
{
	public static void main (String args [])
	{
	boolean j=true;
	j=j & !true;
	System.out.println(j);
	}
}
```

Puzzle 113:

```
class Puzzle113
{
	public static void main (String args [])
	{
	Boolean j =true;
	System.out.println (j);
	}
}
```

Puzzle 114:

```
class Puzzle114
{
	public static void main (String args [])
	{
	int j=0x12;
	if (j==12)
	System.out.println (j);
	}
}
```

Puzzle 115:

```
class Puzzle115
{
	public static void main (String args [])
	{
		int j=0;
		if (j)
		System.out.println (j);
		else
		System.out.println ("J is not zero");
	}
}
```

Puzzle 116:

```
class Puzzle116
{
	public static void main (String args [])
	{
		int j=1;
		if (!j)
		System.out.println ("j is zero");
		else
		System.out.println ("J is not zero");
	}
}
```

Puzzle 117:

```
class Puzzle117
{
	public static void main (String args [])
	{
```

```
        System.out.println (3>>>1);
        }
}
```

Puzzle 118:

```
class Puzzle118
{
        public static void main (String args [])
        {
                boolean j=true;
                if (! j)
                System.out.println ("j is true");
                else
                System.out.println ("J is not true");
        }
}
```

Puzzle 119:

```
class Puzzle119
{
        public static void main (String args [])
        {
        synchronized int j =4;
        System.out.println(j);
        }
}
```

Puzzle 120:

```
class Puzzle120
{
        boolean krack, jack;
```

```
        Puzzle120 (boolean j )
        {
        krack =j;
        jack =!j;
        }

        public static void main (String args [])
        {
        boolean salt, sugar;
        Puzzle120 P120 =new Puzzle120 (true);
        if (P120.krack==true){
        salt =true; sugar=!salt;}
        else{
        salt =true; sugar=!sugar;}
        System.out.println(salt+" "+sugar);
        }
}
```

Puzzle 121:

```
class Puzzle121
{
        public static void main (String args [])
        {
        int j=4, k=5;
        for(j=j j<j+k; j++)
        System.out.println(j);
        }
}
```

Puzzle 122:

```
class Puzzle122
{
```

```
        boolean krack, jack;
        Puzzle122 (boolean j){
        krack =j;
        jack =! j;
        }

        public static void main (String args []) {
        boolean salt=true, sugar=true;Puzzle122 P122
        =new Puzzle122 (true);
        if (P122.krack==true){
        salt =true; sugar=! salt;}
        else{
        salt =true; sugar=!sugar;}
        System.out.println (salt+" "+sugar);}
}
```

Puzzle 123:

```
class Puzzle123
{
        public static void main (String args [])
        {
        int k=6;
        if(k--==5)
                System.out.println("I is five");
        else
                System.out.println(k);
        }
}
```

Puzzle 124:

```
class Puzzle124
{
```

```
        public static void main (String args [])
        {
        int k=6;
        if(-k==-6)
                System.out.println("k is 6");
        }
}
```

Puzzle 125:

```
class Puzzle125
{
        public static void main (String args [])
        {
        int k=8;
        if(- --k==-7)
                System.out.println ("k is 6");
        }
}
```

Puzzle 126:

```
class Puzzle126
{
        public static void main (String args [])
        {
        int k=9;
        if ((k-=8) ==1)
                System.out.println ("k is 1");
        }
}
```

Puzzle 127:

```
class Puzzle127
{
        public static void main (String args [])
        {
        int k=-8;
        System.out.println ("value of K is "+k);
        }
}
```

Puzzle 128:

```
class Puzzle128
{
        public static void main (String args [])
        {
        int k=-8;
        System.out.println(k+(-k));
        }
}
```

Puzzle 129:

```
class Puzzle129
{
        public static void main (String args [])
        {
        for (int k=0;k<10;k++)
        System.out.println("Value of i is "+k/(-k));
        }
}
```

Puzzle 130:

```
class Puzzle130
{
        public static void main (String args []) {
        boolean com=true;
        System.out.println("Complex"+ (Com/com));}
}
```

Puzzle 131:

```
class Puzzle131
{
        public static void main (String args []) {
        finally int b=4;
        System.out.println("Output is" + b);}
}
```

Puzzle 132:

```
class Puzzle132
{
        public static void main (String args []) {
        int a=4;
        switch(a){
                case 1:System.out.println("One"); break;
                case 2:System.out.println("Two"); break;
                case 3:System.out.println("Three"); break;}
        }
}
```

Puzzle 133:

```
class Puzzle133
```

```
{
	public static void main (String args []) {
	int a=4;
	switch (3) {
	case 1: System.out.println ("1"); break;
	case 2: System.out.println ("2"); break;
	case 3: System.out.println("3"); break;
	case a: System.out.println ("4"); break;
	}
	}
}
```

Puzzle 134:

```
class Puzzle134
{
	public static void main (String args []) {
	byte a=4;
	switch(a+2){
		case4:System.out.println("four"); break;
		case 5:System.out.println("Five"); break;
		case 6:System.out.println("Sixth"); break;
	}
	}
}
```

Puzzle 135:

```
class Puzzle135
{
	public static void main (String args []) {
	byte a=4;
	final int b=3;
	switch(a){
```

```
                case 3:System.out.println("three"); break;
                case b: System.out.println("b"); break;
        }
        }
}
```

Puzzle 136:

```
class Puzzle136
{
        public static void main (String args []) {
        byte a=4;
        final int b=3;
        switch (a){
                case 4: System.out.println("four"); break;
                case b: System.out.println("b"); break;
        }
        }
}
```

Puzzle 137:

```
class Puzzle137
{
        public static void main (String args []) {
        final int a=3,b=2;
        int c=a+b;
        System.out.println(c);
        }
}
```

Puzzle 138:

```
class Puzzle138
```

```
{
        public static void main (String args [])
        {
        short a=3,b=2;
        final short c=2;
        switch(a-1)
        {
        case c: System.out.println("C value is 2");
        break;
        case a-1: System.out.println("Same C val");
        break;
        }
        }
}
```

Puzzle 139:

```
class Puzzle139
{
        public static void main (String args []) {

        float a =1.0f;
        switch (a)
        {
        case 1.0: System.out.println ("1.0 ");
        break;
        case 1: System.out.println ("1");
        break;
        case 1.0f: System.out.println ("1.0f ");
        break;
        }
        }
}
```

Puzzle 140:

```
class Puzzle140
{
        static boolean b;
        public static void main(String args[])
        {
        switch(b)
        {
        case true: System.out.println("True"); break;
        case false: System.out.println("True"); break;
        }
        }
}
```

Puzzle 141:

```
class Puzzle141
{
        static int a;
        public static void main (String args[])
        {
        switch (a){
        case 0: System.out.println("0"); break;
        case 1: System.out.println("1"); break;
        }
        }
}
```

Puzzle 142:

```
class Puzzle142
{
        public static void main (String args [])
```

```
        {
        boolean b=3>2;
        if (b)
                System.out.println (“3>2”);
        else
                System.out.println (“2>3”);
        }
}
```

Puzzle 143:

```
class Puzzle143
{
        int b;
        public static void main (String args [])
        {
        Puzzle143 P143 = new Puzzle143();
        P143.b=2;
        switch (P143.b){
        case 1: System.out.println(“1”); break;
        case 2: System.out.println(“2”); break;
        default: System.out.println(“U”); break;
        }
        }
}
```

Puzzle 144:

```
class Puzzle144
{
        int a;
        Puzzle144 (int b) {
        a=b;
        }
```

```
        public static void main (String args [])
        {
        Puzzle144 P144A = new Puzzle144(2);
        Puzzle144 P144B = P144A;
        System.out.println (P144A.a);
        }
}
```

Puzzle 145:

```
class Puzzle145
{
        public static void main (String args [])
        {
        public int a;
        a=3;
        System.out.println (a);
        }
}
```

Puzzle 146:

```
class Puzzle146
{
        public static void main (String args [])
        {
        double j =0x1;
        System.out.println (j);
        }
}
```

Puzzle 147:

```
class Puzzle147
```

```
{
        public static void main (String args []){
        int a;
        finally{
        int a=4;
        System.out.println(a);}
        a=5;
        System.out.println(a);}
}
```

Puzzle 148:

```
class Puzzle148
{
        public static void main (String args [])
        {
                int a=4;
                if(a>3)
                {
                System.out.println (a);
                a--;
                continue ;
                }
        }
}
```

Puzzle 149:

```
class Puzzle149
{
        public static void main (String args [])
        {
                int a=3;
                do{
```

```
                a--;
                System.out.println (a);
                a--;
                }while(a>0);
        }
}
```

Puzzle 150:

```
class Puzzle150
{
        public static void main (String args [])
        {
                int a =4+5%3;
                do{
                a++;
                System.out.println(a+",");
                }while(a<10);
        }
}
```

Puzzle 151:

```
class Puzzle151A
{
        Puzzle151A ( ) {
        System.out.println ("I am in A");
        }
}

class Puzzle151B extends Puzzle151A
{
        Puzzle151B ( ) {
        System.out.println ("I am in B");
```

```
        }
        public static void main (String args[])
        {
        Puzzle151A P151A = new Puzzle151B ();
        }
}
```

Puzzle 152:

```
class Puzzle152A
{
        Puzzle152A( ) {
        System.out.println ("I am in A");
        }
        public static void main (String args[]){
        Puzzle151A P151A = new Puzzle151A ();
        }
}

class Puzzle151B extends Puzzle151A
{
        Puzzle151B ( ){
        System.out.println ("I am in B");
        }
}
```

Puzzle 153:

```
class Puzzle153A
{
        Puzzle153A () {
        System.out.println ("I am in A");}
        public static void main (String args[]){
        Puzzle153B P153B = new Puzzle153A( );}
}
```

```
class Puzzle153B extends Puzzle153A
{
        Puzzle153B (){
        System.out.println ("I am in B");
        }
}
```

Puzzle 154:

```
class Puzzle154A
{
        Puzzle154A (){
        System.out.println ("I am in A");}
        void func (){
        System.out.println ("I am in AF");}
}

class Puzzle154B extends Puzzle154A
{
        Puzzle154B (){
        System.out.println ("I am in B");}
        public static void main (String args[]){
        Puzzle154B P154B = new Puzzle154B();
        P154B.func();
        }
}
```

Puzzle 155:

```
class Puzzle155A
{
        void Puzzle155A (){
        System.out.println ("I am in A");}
}
```

```
class Puzzle155B extends Puzzle155A
{
        public static void main (String args[]){
        Puzzle155B P155B = new Puzzle155B();
        }
}
```

Puzzle 156:

```
class Puzzle156A{
        void Puzzle156A (){
        System.out.println ("I am in A");}
        Puzzle156A (){
        System.out.println ("I am in processing of creating A");}
}

class Puzzle156B extends Puzzle156A{
        Puzzle156B(){
        System.out.println ("I am in B");}
        public static void main (String args[]){
        Puzzle156B P156B = new Puzzle156B();
        }
}
```

Puzzle 157:

```
class Puzzle157A{
        void Puzzle157A (){
        System.out.println ("I am in A");}
        public static void main (String args[]){
        Puzzle157A P157A = new Puzzle157A();
        }
}
```

```
class Puzzle157B extends Puzzle157A{
        Puzzle157B(){
        System.out.println ("I am in B");}
        public static void main (String args[]){
        Puzzle157B P157B = new Puzzle157B();}
}
```

Puzzle 158:

```
class Puzzle158A{
        void private A(){
        System.out.println("Private A()");
        }
}

class Puzzle158B extends Puzzle158A{
        public static void main (String args[]){
        Puzzle158B P158B =new Puzzle158A();
        }
}
```

Puzzle 159:

```
class Puzzle159A{
        void fun(){
        System.out.println("Fun with A");
        }

}
class Puzzle159B extends Puzzle159A{
        void fun(){
        System.out.println("Fun with B");
        }
        public static void main (String args[]){
```

```
        super.fun();
        }
}
```

Puzzle 160:

```
class Puzzle160A{
        void fun(){
        System.out.println("Fun with A");
        }
        }

class Puzzle160B extends Puzzle160A{
        void fun(){
        System.out.println("Fun with B");
        super.fun();
        }
        public static void main (String args[]){
        Puzzle160B P160B = new Puzzle160B();
        P160Bfun();
        }
}
```

Puzzle 161:

```
class Puzzle161A {
        void fun(){
        System.out.println("Fun with A");}
}
class Puzzle161B extends Puzzle161A{
        Puzzle161B(){
        System.out.println("Fun with B");}
}
class Puzzle161C extends Puzzle161B {
```

```
        public static void main (String args[]){
        Puzzle161C P161C = new Puzzle161C();
        }
}
```

Puzzle 162:

```
abstract class Puzzle162A {
        Puzzle162A ()
        {
        System.out.println ("I am in A");
        }
        int fun ();
}

class Puzzle162B extends Puzzle162A
{
        Puzzle162B ( )
        {
        System.out.println ("I am in B");
        }
        private int fun ( )
        {
        System.out.println("Yeah! it is a private");
        return 0;
        }
        public static void main (String args[])
        {
        Puzzle162A P162A = new Puzzle162A( );
        P162A.fun( );
        Puzzle162B P162B = new Puzzle162B();
        P162B.fun( );
        Puzzle162B P162C = new Puzzle162A();
        P162C.fun( );
        }
}
```

Puzzle 163:

```
abstract class Puzzle163A {
        int fun (int i )
        {
        System.out.println ("I am in A");
        }
}

class Puzzle163B {
        int fun ( ){
        System.out.println ("I am in A");
        }
        public static void main(String args[])
        {
        Puzzle163B P163B = new Puzzle163B();
        P163B.fun();
        P163B.fun(1);
        }
}
```

Puzzle 164:

```
class Puzzle164A{
        final int fun(){
        System.out.println("Function is in A");
        }
}

class Puzzle164B extends Puzzle164A {
        int fun(){
        System.out.println("Function is in B");
        }
        public static void main (String args []){
```

```
        Puzzle164B P164B =new Puzzle164B();
        System.out.println (" "+P164B.fun());
        }
}
```

Puzzle 165:

```
class Puzzle165A{
        int fun();
}
class Puzzle165B extends Puzzle165A {
        int fun(){
        System.out.println("Function is in B");
        }
        public static void main (String args []){
        Puzzle165B P165B =new Puzzle165B();
        System.out.println (" "+P165B.fun());
        }
}
```

Puzzle 166:

```
class Puzzle166A {
        private Puzzle166A(){
        System.out.println("Puzzling");
        }
}
class Puzzle166B extend Puzzle166A{
        public static void main(String args[]){
        System.out.println("Testing");
        }
}
```

Puzzle 167:

```
class Puzzle167{
        private Puzzle167(){
        System.out.println("Puzzling");
        }
        public static void main(String args[]){
        System.out.println("Testing");
        }
}
```

Puzzle 168:

```
class Puzzle168{
        final Puzzle168(){
        System.out.println("Puzzling");
        }
        public static void main(String args[]){
        System.out.println("Testing");
        }
}
```

Puzzle 169:

```
class Puzzle169A{
        public static void main(){
        System.out.println("Main of Puzzle169A");
        }
}

class Puzzle169B extends Puzzle169A{
        public static void main(String args[]){
        System.out.println("Testing");
        main();}
}
```

Puzzle 170:

```
class Puzzle170A{
        Puzzle170A(){
        System.out.println("Clear A");}
        Puzzle170A(int i){
        this();
        System.out.println("Clearing A in" + i);}
}

class Puzzle170B extends Puzzle170A{
        Puzzle170B(){
        super();
        System.out.println("Clearing B" );}
        Puzzle170B(int i){
        this();
        System.out.println("B has" + I );}
        public static void main(String args[]){
        Puzzle170B P170B =new Puzzle170B(2);
        }
}
```

Puzzle 171:

```
class Puzzle171{
        Puzzle171()
        {
        System.out.println("Clear A");
        }
        Puzzle171(int i)
        {
        System.out.println("Clearing A in" + i);
        this();
        }
```

```
        public static void main(String args[])
        {
        Puzzle171 P171 =new Puzzle171(1);
        }
}
```

Puzzle 172:

```
class Puzzle172
{
        private Puzzle172 ()
        {
        System.out.println("A is made Private");
        }
        public static void main(String args[])
        {
        Puzzle172 P172 = new Puzzle172 ()
        }
}
```

Puzzle 173:

```
Class Puzzle173A{
        Puzzle173A(int a){
        System.out.println("A has" + a);
        }
}

Class Puzzle173A extends Puzzle173B{
        Puzzle173B(){
        System.out.println("In Puzzle173B" );
        }
        public static void main(String args[]){
        Puzzle173B =new Puzzle173B();
        }
}
```

Puzzle 174:

```
class Puzzle174A{
        Puzzle174A(){
        System.out.println("In Puzzle P174A");
        }
}

class Puzzle174B extends Puzzle174A
{
        Puzzle174B(int a){
        super();
        System.out.println("In Puzzle174B");
        }
        public static void main(String args[]){
        Puzzle174B P174B =new Puzzle174B(2);
        }
}
```

Puzzle 175:

```
class Puzzle175
{
        public static void main(String args[])
        {
        String s =new String("Java") ;
        s=s+ "is Green";
        System.out.println(s);
        }
}
```

Puzzle 176:

```
class Puzzle176
```

```
{
        public static void main(String args[])
        {
        String s =new String("Java") ;
        s.append("XYZ");
        System.out.println(s);
        }
}
```

Puzzle 177:

```
class Puzzle177
{
        public static void main(String args[])
        {
        String s =new String("Lava") ;
        String x = null;
        X=s.reverse();
        System.out.println(s);}
}
```

Puzzle 178:

```
class Puzzle178
{
        public static void main(String args[])
        {
        String s = new String("Lava") ;
        StringBuffer a =s;
        }
}
```

Puzzle 179:

```
class Puzzle179
{
	public static void main(String args[])
	{
	StringBuffer s = new StringBuffer("Lava");
	String a =s;
	}
}
```

Puzzle 180:

```
class Puzzle180
{
	public static void main(String args[])
	{
	StringBuffer s = new String("Lava");
	}
}
```

Puzzle 181:

```
class Puzzle181
{
	public static void main(String args[])
	{
	StringBuffer s = new StringBuffer("Lava");
	s.reverse();
	System.out.println(s);
	s+="from java";
	System.out.println(s);
	}
}
```

Puzzle 182:

```
class Puzzle182
{
        public static void main(String args[])
        {
        StringBuffer s = new StringBuffer("Lava");
        s.append ("Kawa");
        System.out.println(s);
        }
}
```

Puzzle 183:

```
class Java
{
        public static void main(String args[]){
        Java Java= new Java();
        System.out.println(Java);
        System.out.println(args[0]);
        }}
```

Puzzle 184:

```
class Puzzle184
{
        public static void main(String args[]){
        StringBuffer s = new StringBuffer("Lava");
        String s1= new String("Kawa");
        s.append(s1);
        s1+=s;
        System.out.println(s1);
        }
}
```

Puzzle 185:

```
class Puzzle185
{
	public static void main(String args[]){
	String s = new String ("Lava");
	s.append(3.14);
	System.out.println(s);
	}
}
```

Puzzle 186:

```
class Puzzle186
{
	public static void main(String args[]){
	String s = new String ("Lava");
	s+= 3.14;
	System.out.println(s);
	}
}
```

Puzzle 187:

```
class Puzzle187
{
	public static void main(String args[])
	{
	StringBuffer s = new StringBuffer ("Java");
	s.append(s);
	System.out.println(s);
	}
}
```

Puzzle 188:

```
class Puzzle188
{
        public static void main(String args[])
        {
        StringBuffer s = new StringBuffer ("Java");
        s.reverse();
        System.out.println(s);
        }
}
```

Puzzle 189:

```
class Puzzle189{
        public static void main(String args[]){
        StringBuffer s = new StringBuffer ("Java");
        s.toString();
        System.out.println(s);
        }}
```

Puzzle 190:

```
final class Puzzle190
{
        public static void main(String args[]){
        Puzzle190 P190 =new Puzzle190();
        System.out.println("Puzzle190");
        }
}
```

Puzzle 191:

```
final class Puzzle191A
```

```
{
        int a;
}

class Puzzle191B extends Puzzle191A{
        public static void main(String args[]){
        Puzzle191A P191A = new Puzzle191A();
        }
}
```

Puzzle 192:

```
class Puzzle192{
        public static void main(String args[]){
        StringBuffer s = new StringBuffer("Lava");
        s.insert(3,"java");
        System.out.println(s);
        }
}
```

Puzzle 193:

```
class Puzzle193{
        public static void main(String args[]){
        System.out.println(Math.PI);
        System.out.println(Math.ceil(Math.PI));
        }
}
```

Puzzle 194:

```
class Puzzle194{
        public static void main(String args[]){
        int x=4;
```

```
        System.out.println(Math.ceil(x));
        }
}
```

Puzzle 195:

```
class Puzzle195{
        public static void main(String args[]){
        Float F =new Float("3.14f");
        float f=F;
        System.out.println(f+" "+F);}
}
```

Puzzle 196

```
class Puzzle196{
        public static void main(String args[]){
        Float F =new Float("3.14f");
        float f=F.floatValue (F);
        System.out.println(f+" "+F);}
}
```

Puzzle 197

```
class Puzzle197{
        public static void main(String args[])
        {
        Float f=Float.valueOf("3.14f");
        System.out.println(f+" ");
        }
}
```

Puzzle 198:

```
class Puzzle198{
        public static void main(String args[])
        {
        Float f=Float.valueOf(3.14);
```

```
        System.out.println(f.toString());
        }
}
```

Puzzle 199:

```
class Puzzle199{
        public static void main(String args[])
        {
        Double d =new Double(3.14);
        Float f= (Float)d;
        System.out.println(f.toString());
        }
}
```

Puzzle 200:

```
class Puzzle200{
        public static void main(String args[]){
        float f =3.14f;
        Float F =new Float (f);
        System.out.println(F);
        }
}
```

Puzzle 201:

```
class Puzzle201{
        public static void main(String args[])
        {
        Puzzle201 P01A =new Puzzle201();
        Puzzle201 P01B = new Puzzle201();
        System.out.println(P01A.equals(P01B));
        }
}
```

Puzzle 202:

```
class Puzzle202{
        public static void main(String args[])
        {
        Puzzle202 P02A =new Puzzle202();
        Puzzle202 P02B = new Puzzle202();
        System.out.println(P02A.equals(P02B)& P02B.equals(P02A));
        }
}
```

Puzzle 203:

```
class Puzzle203{
        public static void main(String args[])
        {
        Puzzle203 P03A =new Puzzle203();
        Puzzle203 P03B = P03A;
        System.out.println(P03A.equals(P03B));
        }
}
```

Puzzle 204:

```
class Puzzle204{
        class IPuzzle204{
        public static void main(String args[])
        {
        System.out.println("In Puzzle204");
        }
        }
}
```

Puzzle 205:

```
class Puzzle205{
        public static void main(String args[])
        {
        System.out.println("Out of P205");
        }
class IPuzzle205{
        IPuzzle205(){
        System.out.println("In of P205");
        }
        }
}
```

Puzzle 206:

```
class Puzzle206{
        IPuzzle206 IP06= new IPuzzle206();
        public static void main(String args[])
        {

        System.out.println("Out of P206");
        }
class IPuzzle206{
        IPuzzle206(){
        System.out.println("In of P206");
        }
        }
}
```

Puzzle 207:

```
class Puzzle207A
{
```

```
        public static void main(String args[])
        {
        Puzzle207A P07A= new Puzzle207A();
        }
        class Puzzle207B
        {
        Puzzle207B()
        {
        System.out.println("In of P207");
        }
        }
}
```

Puzzle 208:

```
interface Cook{
        public void Cook();
}
class Puzzle208
{
        public static void main(String args[])
        {
        Cook C= new Cook();
        C.Cook();
        }
}
```

Puzzle 209:

```
interface Cook{
        public void Cook(){
        System.out.println("Cooking");
        }
        void cook_it();
}
```

```
class Puzzle209 implements Cook
{
        Puzzle209(){
        System.out.println("I am in Testing Cooks");
        }
        public static void main(String args[])
        {
        Cook C= new Puzzle209 ();
        C.Cook();
        }
}
```

Puzzle 210:

```
class Puzzle210{
        public static void main(String args[]){
        int a[]=new int [4];
        int i;
        for (i=0;i<a.length;i++){
        a[i]=i;
        System.out.print(a[i]+" ");
        }
        }
}
```

Puzzle 211:

```
class Puzzle211{
        public static void main(String args[]){
        int a[] =new int [4];
        int i;
        for (i=0;i<a.length;i++){
        System.out.print(a[i]+" ");
        }
        }
}
```

Puzzle 212:

```
class Puzzle212{
        public static void main(String args[]){
        int a[] =new int [4];
        byte i;
        for (i=0;i<a.length;i++){
        System.out.print(a[i]+" ");}
        }
}
```

Puzzle 213:

```
interface Cook{
        void cookIt();
}

class P213ck_Veg implements Cook
{
        P213ck_Veg(){
        System.out.println("I am in Testing Cooks");}
        void cookIt(){
        System.out.println("Ready for cooking");}
        public static void main(String args[])
        {
        P213ck_Veg P213cV=new P213ck_Veg();
        }
}
```

Puzzle 214:

```
interface Cook{
        void cookIt();
}
```

```
class P214ck_Veg implements Cook{
        P214ck_Veg(){
        System.out.println("I am in Testing Cooks");}
        public void cookIt(){
        System.out.println("Ready for cooking");}
        public static void main(String args[]){
        P214ck_Veg P214cV=new P214ck_Veg();
        }
}
```

Puzzle 215:

```
class Puzzle215 {
        public static void main(String args[])
        {
        final int a=5;
        int arr[] =new int[5];
        int i;
        for(i=0;i<4;i++)
        arr[i]=i;
        arr[4]=a;
        for(i=0;i<4;i++)
        arr[i]=arr[i-1]+arr[i+1];
        for(i=0;i<5;i++)
        System.out.print(arr[i]+" ");
        }
}
```

Puzzle 216:

```
class Puzzle216 {
        public static void main(String args[])
        {
        final int a=5;
```

```
        int arr[] =new int[2];
        arr[0]=a;
        arr[1]=a+3;
        arr[1]=arr[0]+arr[1];
        System.out.print(arr[1]);
        }
}
```

Puzzle 217:

```
class Puzzle217 {
        public static void main(String args[])
        {
        int a =3;
        static int arr[] =new int[a];
        System.out.println(arr[1]+arr[2]);
        }
}
```

Puzzle 218:

```
class Puzzle218 {
        public static void main(String args[])
        {
        String s = "Good Problems";
        System.out.println("["+s+"]");
        }
}
```

Puzzle 219:

```
class Puzzle219{
        public static void main(String args[])
        {
```

```
        String s =new String("Java");
        System.out.println(s.indexOf('a'));
        }
}
```

Puzzle 220:

```
class Puzzle220
{
        public static void main(String args[])
        {
        String s =new String("Java");
        s.touppercase();
        System.out.println(s);
        System.out.println(s.indexOf('a'));
        }
}
```

Puzzle 221:

```
class Puzzle221
{
        protected int a;
        public static void main(String args[])
        {
        Puzzle221 P221 =new Puzzle221();
        P221.a =4;
        P221.fun(1);
        System.out.println(P221.a);
        }
        void fun(int a)
        {
        System.out.println(a);
        }
}
```

Puzzle 222:

```
class Puzzle222{
        public static void main(String args[]){
        String s, r;
        s=" ";
        r=" ";
        if(s==r)
        System.out.println("empty string");
        else
        System.out.println("null string");
        }
}
```

Puzzle 223:

```
class Puzzle223{
        public static void main(String args[]){
        String s;
        char c[] ={'a','b','c','d','e','f'};
        s=new String(c);
        System.out.println(s);
        }
}
```

Puzzle 224:

```
class Puzzle224{
        public static void main(String args[]){
        String s;
        byte b[] ={1,2,3,4,5};
        s=new String(c);
        System.out.println(s);
        }
}
```

Puzzle 225:

```
class Puzzle225
{
	public static void main(String args[])
	{
	char c1[] ={1,2,3,4,5};
	String s;
	s=new String(c1);
	System.out.println(s);
	}
}
```

Puzzle 226:

```
class Puzzle226
{
	public static void main(String args[])
	{
	char d[]= {'a', 'c', 1,'a',3 };
	String s =new String(d,0,3);
	System.out.println(s);
	}
}
```

Puzzle 227:

```
class Puzzle227
{
	public static void main(String args[]){
	int a=1;
	String S ="Hai"+(a+1)+"Java";
	System.out.println(S);
	}
}
```

Puzzle 228:

```
class Puzzle228
{
        public static void main(String args[])
        {
        Puzzle228 P228= new Puzzle228():
        String S =”Testing”+P228;
        System.out.println(S);
        }
}
```

Puzzle 229:

```
class Puzzle229
{
        public static void main(String args[])
        {
        Puzzle228 P228= new Puzzle228():
        String S =”Testing”+P228;
        System.out.println(S);
        }
        public String toString()
        {
        return “ is a fun”;
        }
}
```

Puzzle 230:

```
class Puzzle230
{
        public static void main(String args[])
        {
```

```
        Puzzle229 P229 = new Puzzle229();
        String S = P229;
        }
        public String toString()
        {
        return " is a fun";
        }
}
```

Puzzle 231:

```
class Puzzle231
{
        public static void main(String args[])
        {
        Puzzle229 P229 = new Puzzle229();
        String s ="s is greater";
        String s1 ="s1 is greater";
        if(s>s1)
        System.out.println(s);
        else if (s1>s)
        System.out.println(s1);
        else
        System.out.println("None is Greater");
        }
}
```

Puzzle 232:

```
class Puzzle232
{
        public static void main(String args[])
        {
        StringBuffer sb = new StringBuffer("Java");
```

```
        System.out.println(sb.capacity());
        }
}
```

Puzzle 233:

```
class Puzzle233
{
        public static void main(String args[])
        {
        String S =”JAVA”;
        char c =S.charAt(3);
        System.out.println(c);
        }
}
```

Puzzle 234:

```
class Puzzle234
{
        int a=8;
        public static void main(String args[])
        {
        System.out.println(this.a);
        }
}
```

Puzzle 235:

```
class Puzzle235A{
        int a, b;}

class Puzzle235B extends Puzzle235A{
        int c, d;
```

```
        Puzzle235B(int a, int b, int c, int d){
        this.a=a;
        this.b=b;
        this.c=d;}
}

class Puzzle235{
        public static void main(String args[]){
        Puzzle235A P235A = new Puzzle235B(1,2,3,4);
        System.out.println(P235A.d+ P235A.c);}
}
```

Puzzle 236:

```
class Puzzle236A{
        int a, b;}

class Puzzle236B extends Puzzle236A{
        int c, d;
        Puzzle236B(int a, int b){
        this.a=a;
        this.b=b;
        }
}

class Puzzle236{
        public static void main(String args[]){
        Puzzle236A P236A = new Puzzle236B(1,2);
        System.out.println(P236A.a+ P236A.b);}
}
```

Puzzle 237:

```
class Puzzle237A
```

```
{
        int a, b;
}

class Puzzle237B extends Puzzle237A
{
        int c, d;
        Puzzle237B(int a, int b){
        super.a=a;
        super.b=b;
        }
}

class Puzzle237
{
        public static void main(String args[])
        {
        Puzzle237A P237A = new Puzzle237B(1,2);
        System.out.println(P236A.a+ P236A.b);
        }
}
```

Puzzle 238:

```
class Puzzle238
{
        int a,b;
        Puzzle238(){
        a=0;
        b=0;
        }
        public static void main(String args[])
        {
        Puzzle238 P238[] = new Puzzle238[4];
```

```
        P238[0].a=4;
        P238[0].b=5;
        }
}
```

Puzzle 239:

```
class Puzzle239
{
        int a,b;
        Puzzle239(){
        a=0;
        b=0;
        }
        public static void main(String args[])
        {
        Puzzle239 P239[] = new Puzzle239[4];
        P239[0] =new Puzzle239();
        P239[0].a=4;
        P239[0].b=5;
        System.out.println(P239[0].a+ P239[0].b);}
}
```

Puzzle 240:

```
class Puzzle240A{
        int a,b;}

class Puzzle240B extends Puzzle240A {
        private int b,c;
}

class Puzzle240{
        public static void main(String args[]){
```

```
        Puzzle240A P240= new Puzzle240B();
        P240.a=3;
        P240.b=4;
        System.out.println(P240.a+ P240.b);
        }
}
```

Puzzle 241:

```
class Puzzle241A{
        void Ptest(){
        System.out.println("Testing for P241");
        }
}

class Puzzle241B extends Puzzle241A {
        private void Ptest(){
        System.out.println("Testing for P241");
        }
}

class Puzzle241{
        public static void main(String args[]){
        Puzzle241A P241= new Puzzle241B();
        P241.Ptest();
        }
}
```

Puzzle 242:

```
class Puzzle242{
        static int a[] =new int [5];
        public static void main(String args[]){
        for (int i=0;i<a.length;i++)
```

```
                System.out.println(a[i]);
        }
}
```

Puzzle 243:

```
class Puzzle243{
        public static void main(String args[]){
        int a[] ={1,2,3,4,5};
        for (int i=0;i<a.length;i++)
        System.out.println(a[i]);}
}
```

Puzzle 244:

```
class Puzzle244{
        public static void main(String args[]){
        static int a =4;
        System.out.println(a);
        }
}
```

Puzzle 245:

```
class Puzzle245
{
        public static void main(String args[])
        {
        String s[] = new String[5];
        System.out.println(s[0]+ s[1]+ s[2]+ s[3]+ s[4]);
        }
}
```

Puzzle 246:

```
class Puzzle246A{
        void SendObject(Puzzle246B P246B){
        System.out.println("In B language");
        }
        void SendObject(Puzzle246C P246C){
        System.out.println("In C language");
        }
        public static void main(String args[]){
        Puzzle246A P246A = new Puzzle246A();
        Puzzle246B P246B = new Puzzle246B();
        Puzzle246C P246C = new Puzzle246C();
        P246A. SendObject(P246B);
        P246A. SendObject(P246C);
        }
}

class Puzzle246B{
}
class Puzzle246C extends Puzzle246B{
}
```

Puzzle 247:

```
class Puzzle247
{
        public static void main(String args[])
        {
        Puzzle247A P247A = new Puzzle247A();
        P247A. SendObject(P247A);
        Puzzle247B P247B = new Puzzle247B();
        P247A. SendObject(P247B);
        Puzzle247C P247C = new Puzzle247C();
```

```
        P247A. SendObject(P247C);
        }
}

class Puzzle247A
{
        void SendObject(Object P247){
        System.out.println("In Object language");
        }
        void SendObject(Puzzle247B P247B){
        System.out.println("In B language");
        }
        void SendObject(Puzzle247C P247C){
        System.out.println("In C language");
        }
}

class Puzzle247B
{
}
class Puzzle247C extends Puzzle247B
{
}
```

Puzzle 248:

```
class Puzzle248
{
        public static void main(String args[])
        {
        Puzzle248A P248A = new Puzzle248A();
        P248A. SendObject(P248A);
        Puzzle248B P248B = new Puzzle248B();
        P248A. SendObject(P248B);
```

```
        Puzzle248C P248C = new Puzzle248C();
        P248A. SendObject(P248C);
        }
}

class Puzzle248A
{
        void SendObject(Object P248)
        {
        System.out.println("In Object language");
        }
        void SendObject(Puzzle248B P248B)
        {
        System.out.println("In B language");
        }
}

class Puzzle248B
{
}
class Puzzle248C extends Puzzle248B
{
}
```

Puzzle 249:

```
class Puzzle249A
{
        int a;
        Puzzle249A(int a){
        this.a=a;
        }
        int geta(){
        return a;
        }
}
```

```
class Puzzle249
{
        public static void main(String args[]){
        int test=new Puzzle249A(2).geta();
        System.out.println(test);
        }
}
```

Puzzle 250:

```
class Puzzle250A{
        int a;
        protected void finalize(){
        System.out.println("Finalized");}
}
class Puzzle250B extends Puzzle250A{
}
class Puzzle250C{
        public static void main(String args[]){
        Puzzle250B P250B = new Puzzle250B();
        P250B=null;
        }
}
```

Puzzle 251:

```
class Puzzle251A{
        static int a=0;
        Puzzle251A(){
        A++;
        }
}
```

```
class Puzzle251B{
        public static void main(String args[]){
        new Puzzle251A();
        new Puzzle251A();
        System.out.println(Puzzle251A.a);
        }
}
```

Puzzle 252:

```
class Puzzle252A{
        int a=1;
        static Puzzle252A(){
        System.out.println("Creating A");
        }
}

class Puzzle252B{
        public static void main(String args[]){
        Puzzle252A P252A=new Puzzle252A();
        }
}
```

Puzzle 253:

```
class Puzzle253A{
        int a;
        protected Puzzle253A(){}
}

class Puzzle253B{
        Puzzle253B(){
        super();
        }
```

```
}
class Puzzle253C extends Puzzle253B{
}
```

Puzzle 254:

```
class Puzzle254A{
        int a;
        protected Puzzle254A(){
        System.out.println("Protect your Object");
        }
}

class Puzzle254B extends Puzzle254A{
        Puzzle254B(){
        super();
        }
        public static void main(String args[]){
        Puzzle254B P254B = new Puzzle254B();
        }
}
```

Puzzle 255:

```
class Puzzle255A{
        int a;
        protected Puzzle255A(){
        System.out.println("Protect your Object");
        }
        Puzzle255A(int a){
        System.out.println("Protect your Object in "+a);
        }
}
```

```
class Puzzle255B extends Puzzle255A{
	Puzzle255B(int a){
	}
	public static void main(String args[]){
	Puzzle255B P255B = new Puzzle255B(2);
	}
}
```

Puzzle 256:

```
class Puzzle256A{
	int a;
	Puzzle256A(int a){
	System.out.println("Protect your Object in "+a);}
}

class Puzzle256B extends Puzzle256A{
	Puzzle256B(int a){super(a);}
	public static void main(String args[]){
	Puzzle256B P256B = new Puzzle256B(2);}
	}
```

Puzzle 257:

```
class Puzzle257A{
	int a;
	private void Tover(){
	System.out.println("Testing is over");
	}
}

class Puzzle257B extends Puzzle257A{
	void Tover(){
	System.out.println("Testing is over :2");
```

```
        }
        public static void main(String args[]){
        Puzzle257A P257A = new Puzzle257B();
        P257A.Tover();
        }
}
```

Puzzle 258:

```
class Puzzle258A{
        int a;
        void Tover(){
        System.out.println("Testing is over");}
}

class Puzzle258B extends Puzzle258A{
        void Tover(){
        System.out.println("Testing is over :2");
        }
        public static void main(String args[]){
        Puzzle258A P258A = new Puzzle258B();
        P258A.Tover();
        }
}
```

Puzzle 259:

```
class Puzzle259{
        Puzzle259(){
        this();
        System.out.println("A is Flower");
        }
}
```

Puzzle 260:

```
class Puzzle259{
	Puzzle259(){
	super();
	System.out.println("A is Flower");
	}
}
```

Puzzle 261:

```
class Puzzle261A{
	int a;
}

class Puzzle261B{
	public static void main(String args[]){
	final Puzzle261A P261A = new Puzzle261A();
	P261A.a=5;
	System.out.println(P261A.a);
	}
}
```

Puzzle 262:

```
class Puzzle262A{
	int a;
}

class Puzzle262B{
	public static void main(String args[]){
	final Puzzle262A P262A = new Puzzle262A();
	P262A.a=5;
	System.out.println(P262A.a);
```

```
        P262A.a =new Puzzle262A();
        }
}
```

Puzzle 263:

```
class Puzzle263{
        public static void main(String args[]){
        int a[]=new int [5];
        int b[]=new int [4];
        int c[]={1,2,3,4};
        int i;
        for (i=0;i<a.length;i++)
        System.out.print(a[i]);
        System.out.println();
        a=c;
        System.out.print(a.length+" ");
        for (i=0;i<a.length;i++)
        System.out.print(a[i]);
        }
}
```

Puzzle 264:

```
class Puzzle264
{
        public static void main(String args[]){
        Puzzle264 P264 =new Puzzle264();
        if(P264 instanceof Object )
        System.out.println("P264 is instance of Object");}
}
```

Puzzle 265:

```
class Puzzle265
{
        public static void main(String args[]){
        Puzzle265 P265;
        if(P265 instanceof Puzzle265)
        System.out.println("P265 is instance of Puzzle265");}
}
```

Puzzle 266:

```
class Puzzle266
{
        public static void main(String args[]){
        Puzzle266 P266[] = new Puzzle266[5];
        if(P266 instanceof Puzzle266)
        System.out.println("P266 is instance of Puzzle266");}
}
```

Puzzle 267:

```
class Puzzle267
{
        public static void main(String args[]){
        Puzzle267 P267[] = new Puzzle267[5];
        if(P267 instanceof Puzzle267[])
        System.out.println("P267 is instance of Puzzle267[]");
        }
}
```

Puzzle 268:

```
class Puzzle268
```

```
{
        public static void main(String args[]){
        Puzzle268 P268[] = new Puzzle268[5];
        P268[0]= new Puzzle268();
        if(P268[0] instanceof Puzzle268)
        System.out.println("P268[0] is instance of Puzzle268");
        }
}
```

Puzzle 269:

```
class Puzzle269
{
        public static void main(String args[]){
        Puzzle269 P269[] = new Puzzle269[5];
        if(P269 instanceof Object)
        System.out.println("P269[0] is instance of Puzzle269");}
}
```

Puzzle 270:

```
class Puzzle270A
{
        Puzzle270A()
        {
        System.out.println("Creating a Puzzle...");
        }
}

class Puzzle270B extends Puzzle270A
{
        public static void main(String args[])
        {
        Puzzle270A P270A[] = new Puzzle270B[5];
```

```
        if(P270A instanceof Puzzle270B[])
        System.out.println("P270A is instance of Puzzle270");
        if(P270A instanceof Puzzle270A[])
        System.out.println("P270A is instance of Puzzle270");
        }
}
```

Puzzle 271:

```
class Puzzle271{
        private void fun(){
        System.out.println("funtest");
        }
        public void fun(){
        System.out.println("funtest");
        }
}
```

Puzzle 272:

```
abstract class Puzzle272A
{
        Puzzle272A(){
        System.out.println("abstract Puzzle272");
        }
}

class Puzzle272B extends Puzzle272A
{
        Puzzle272B(){
        System.out.println("In Puzzle272B");
        }
        public static void main(String args[]){
        Puzzle272A P272A =new Puzzle272B();
        }
}
```

Puzzle 273:

```
abstract class Puzzle273A
{
        static void fun(){
        System.out.println("fun with Puzzle273");
        }
}

class Puzzle273B extends Puzzle273A
{
        public static void main(String args[]){
        fun();
        }
}
```

Puzzle 274:

```
class Puzzle274A{
        static void fun(){
        System.out.println("fun with P274A");
        }
}

class Puzzle274B extends Puzzle274A {

        static void fun(){
        System.out.println("fun with P274B");
        }

        public static void main(String args[]){
        fun();}
}
```

Puzzle 275:

```
class Puzzle275A{
        static void fun(){
        System.out.println("fun with P275A");
        }
}

class Puzzle275B extends Puzzle275A{
        static void fun(){
        super.fun();
        System.out.println("fun with P275B");
        }

        public static void main(String args[]){
        fun();
        }
}
```

Puzzle 276:

```
class Puzzle276
{
        static int a;
        static void fun(int a)
        {
        this.a =a;
        System.out.println("Fun with" + a);
        }
        public static void main(String args[])
        {
        fun(2);
        }
}
```

Puzzle 277:

```
class Puzzle277
{
	public static void fun()
	{
	System.out.println("Fun with P277" );
	}
	public static void main(String args[])
	{
	Puzzle277 P277 =new Puzzle277();
	fun();
	Puzzle277.fun();
	P277.fun();
	}
}
```

Puzzle 278:

```
interface IPuzzle278{
	private int a;
}
class Puzzle278 implements IPuzzle278{
	public static void main(String args[]){
	System.out.println("P278 imp IP278");}
}
```

Puzzle 279:

```
interface IPuzzle279{
	int a=7;
}

class Puzzle279 implements IPuzzle279{
```

```
        public static void main(String args[]){
        System.out.println("P279 imp IP279");
        System.out.println(a);}
}
```

Puzzle 280:

```
interface IPuzzle280{
        int a=7;
}
class Puzzle280 implements IPuzzle280{
        public static void main(String args[]){
        a=a+7;
        System.out.println(a);}
}
```

Puzzle 281:

```
final interface IPuzzle281
{
        void Test_IPuzzle281()
        {
        System.out.println("Hai");
        }
}

class Puzzle281 implements IPuzzle281
{
        public static void main(String args[])
        {
        System.out.println("Hai");
        }
}
```

Puzzle 282:

```
interface IPuzzle282
{
	void Test_IPuzzle282();
}

class Puzzle282 extends IPuzzle282
{
	public static void main(String args[])
	{
	System.out.println("Hai");
	}
}
```

Puzzle 283:

```
interface IPuzzle283{
	static int a;
	void Testing();
}

class Puzzle283 implements IPuzzle283{
	void Testing(){
	System.out.println("Testing");
	}
	public static void main(String args[]){
	System.out.println(a);}
}
```

Puzzle 284:

```
interface IPuzzle284A{
	static int a=1;
```

```
        void Testing();
}

interface IPuzzle284B extends IPuzzle284A{
        static int a=2;


}

class Puzzle284 implements IPuzzle284B{
        public void Testing(){
        System.out.println("Testing");}
        public static void main(String args[]){
        System.out.println(a);
        }
}
```

Puzzle 285:

```
class Puzzle285A{
        int Test1=9; }

class Puzzle285B extends Puzzle285A{
        static int Test1= super.Test1;}

class Puzzle285{
        public static void main(String args[]){
        System.out.println(Puzzle285B.Test1);
        }
}
```

Puzzle 286:

```
class Puzzle286{
        public static void main(String args[]){
```

```
        int r=3,f=9;
        if(0==f%r)
        System.out.println("Zero");
        else
        System.out.println("One");
        }
}
```

Puzzle 287:

```
class Puzzle287{
        public static void main(String args[] = new String[4]){
        System.out.println("NewWay");
        }
}
```

Puzzle 288:

```
interface IPuzzle288A
{
        static int a=1;
        void Testing();
}
interface IPuzzle288B extends IPuzzle288A
{
        static int a=2;


}
class Puzzle288 implements IPuzzle288B, IPuzzle288A
{
        public void Testing(){
        System.out.println("Testing");}
        public static void main(String args[]){
        System.out.println(a);
        }
}
```

Puzzle 289:

```
abstract class Puzzle289
{
	abstract short m1();
	short m2();
}
```

Puzzle 290:

```
class Puzzle290A
{
	short m2(){
	System.out.println("Short in m2");
	return 7;
	}
}

abstract class Puzzle290B extends Puzzle290A
{
	abstract short m2();
}
```

Puzzle 291:

```
abstract class Puzzle291A{
	short m2(){
	System.out.println("Short in m2");
	return 7;
	}
}

abstract class Puzzle291B extends Puzzle291A{
	abstract short m2();
}
```

```
class Puzzle291 extends Puzzle291B{
        public static void main(String args[]){
        Puzzle291 P291 =new Puzzle291();
        System.out.println(P291.m2());
        }
}
```

Puzzle 292:

```
interface IPuzzle292A{
        void Test();
}

interface IPuzzle292B extends IPuzzle292A{
        void Test();
        void Test(int i);
}

abstract class Puzzle292 implements IPuzzle292B{
        public void Test(){
        System.out.println("Testing");
        }
}
```

Puzzle 293:

```
class Puzzle293A{
        class Puzzle293B{
        class Puzzle293C{}
        }
}
```

Puzzle 294:

```
class Puzzle294{
        final static int a;
        static {a=6;}
        public static void main(String args[]){
        System.out.print("Hai" +a);
        }
}
```

Puzzle 295:

```
class Puzzle295{
        final static int a;
        int b;
        static {
        a=6;
        b=a;}
        public static void main(String args[]){
        System.out.print("Hai" +a);
        }
}
```

Puzzle 296:

```
class Puzzle296{
        final static int a=3;
        static {
        a=6;
        }
        public static void main(String args[]){
        System.out.print("Hai" +a);
        }
}
```

Puzzle 297:

```
class Puzzle297{
        static int a=3;
        static {
        a=6;}
        public static void main(String args[]){
        System.out.print("Hai" +a);
        }
}
```

Puzzle 298:

```
class Puzzle298{
        static int a=3;
        static {
        System.out.print("Hai" +a);
        }
        public static void main(String args[]){
        System.out.print("Hai" +a);
        }
}
```

Puzzle 299:

```
class Puzzle299{
        static int a=3;
        static {
        System.out.print("Hai" +a);
        }
        public static void main(String args[]){
        a=9;
        System.out.print("Hai" +a);
        }
}
```

www.ingramcontent.com/pod-product-compliance
Lightning Source LLC
Chambersburg PA
CBHW051248050326
40689CB00007B/1113

* 9 7 8 1 4 6 6 9 8 8 8 5 9 *